The Isle of Smoothies

Max Sandall

ISBN: 1519206739
ISBN-13: 978-1519206732

For Polly.

CONTENTS

Acknowledgments   i

The Isle of Smoothies   3

ACKNOWLEDGMENTS

I would like to thank Rob Bowyer for his fabulous cover art, as well as La Mer (Claire Sandall) for her editing skills. Lastly, I would like to honour the memory of Sir Terry Pratchett: always an inspiration.

THE ISLE OF SMOOTHIES

They called themselves the Council of Greyhounds – the wise, smooth ones who lived far above the forest canopy in their cave.

A fire crackled and sputtered as old, rheumy eyes stared into its heart.

'Matters are getting worse,' said a large greyhound, its voice hollow and echoing among the rock. 'More of our kind are being taken. It seems the Mother's influence has left the island.'

They'd all thought it, yes, and the elder's sullen words spoke to them in turn. The Mother. The human who had passed away only weeks before. She'd kept peace - for the most part - and now she was gone.

The greyhounds' wide, scintillating eyes shared a wordless grief as they remembered. Alice.

'The Lupine Gang have always caused us islanders trouble,' said a brown greyhound, its waxen coat shimmering in the light of the fire. 'But they would never do such a thing under the Mother's influence.'

The hounds nodded their agreement. Kidnapping and for what purpose? Loved ones: family members, friends, significant others. All gone, and taken by that insidious group, the Lupine Gang.

A sandy haired greyhound peered around the circle. 'Well? What are we to do now?'

There was a collective sigh, a dusty, weathered sound full of uncertainty and an almost inevitability.

After a time, the elder turned away from the fire and towards the light of the cave entrance. 'I have chosen my nephew,' he said, 'an ambitious young whippet snapper. I have seen it in the fire. *I have seen it.* I have seen hope.'

The sandy haired greyhound raised her brow. 'You can't possibly mean...'

'Yes.' The elder glared at the hounds, challenging anyone who dared question him. 'I am sending my nephew. I am sending Count Chocula.'

The bloodhound snored beneath the moonlight, a choked and rubbery sound, its jowls flapping in unison.

This particular hound, known as Old Marvin, was – as his name might have suggested – an elderly fellow (or, as the islanders would call someone of his seniority, a dusty pig). He spent his days roaming the island and the undergrowth of the jungle, sniffing out whatever wonderful and mysterious treats lay beneath the decaying leaves and stumps.

Today had yielded a half rotten banana and a tin of tobacco, the contents of which were bone dry, with a taste like sour raisins.

Old Marvin had wondered about that tin. How long had it been there? An item dropped by a soldier, in the days of the Great War, perhaps?

That piece of information had been passed down by the Oracle, an entity rumoured to be living on the furthest part of the island. Beneath the palms and creepers of the jungle lay a wealth of secrets. Supposedly, the Oracle was privy to some of these.

Yet Old Marvin, for all his bumbling years, felt content in sniffing out bananas and other less savoury items. The island could keep its secrets, as far as he was concerned.

But secrets had a way of surfacing, like shoots under dappled light; Old Marvin was about to find that out.

A shadow rose slowly over the bloodhound, blocking the pale moon. Paws hovered over his muzzle, and moments later the hound was gone.

He wasn't the first. And he wouldn't be the last.

Bwalene gazed at the ocean, watching the sun glimmer – dreamlike - against curling waves. It was beautiful, but the scene held no beauty for the Boston terrier. Even the warmth of the sun on her smooth, piebald coat brought no solace: as if she were viewing the world through a window, one in which all feeling lay on the other side.

Bob… her smoothie, her sweetheart. Gone. Another victim of the kidnappings that had swept the island so suddenly. The shock and anxiety had ended up morphing into a hollow, empty sadness. It was an awful state of being, and Bwalene could do nothing to curb it.

'I'll get it thisth time!' Chompy Chew called, as he ran for the stick that arched beneath the cloudless sky. It hit the French bulldog on the side of his bulbous head, and Chompy Chew cursed, his lisp accentuating a rather colourful and sibilant word.

'To me.'

Alfonz - a pug with short, stubby legs - fared no better as the French bulldog flicked his head, the stick soaring skyward then down to the sand. He picked it up with tiny jaws, and through gritted teeth said 'Bwalene?' offering the stick to the glum Boston terrier.

Bwalene stared at it vacantly, leaving an awkward silence. Alfonz pawed at the sand. He was a kind-hearted pug, always wanting the best for others, but he found it difficult to talk to troubled souls. And Bwalene was troubled. Her ping-pong eyes seemed to protrude further than usual.

Chompy Chew came running up to meet them at the edge of the beach. 'It would be sthuper if you joined usth,' he said with alacrity.

But Bwalene only sat there, not feeling the sun on her back, nor the sand between her paws or the rich smell of foliage from the jungle behind her...

A jungle that began to shake and stir, to the surprise of both the Frenchie and the pug.

A black whippet came stumbling out the trees, branches strapped to its iridescent body. It stared at the other dogs in silence, until Alfonz couldn't take the tension.

'I can see you, you know?' he said, taking a step back.

The whippet looked down at its body very carefully. 'Oh,' he said.

This peculiar turn of events did something remarkable in Bwalene's mind. She started to feel... curiosity, and a mix of amusement. What was this strange dog doing, emerging from the jungle covered in twigs and leaves?

'You're not, uhm, you're not members of the Lupine Gang, are you?' said the whippet.

The three looked at each other, perplexed.

'The kidnappersth?' said Chompy Chew, his forehead scrunched. 'Do we look like a gang of kidnappersth?'

The whippet stared at the pug, the French bulldog and the Boston terrier. 'I suppose you don't.' He inspected his paw for no apparent reason. 'I've been sent on a mission, you see.'

'A mission?' said Alfonz, whose scrunched face required no further scrunching.

'That's right,' said the whippet, beaming. 'I've been sent by the Council of Greyhounds on a secret mission.'

'Sthecret...' Chompy Chew wondered what on earth had possessed the council to think this was a good idea.

'My name is Count Chocula,' said the whippet, standing as tall as his bony legs would allow him. 'My mission is to locate the Lupine Gang and retrieve...'

But Bwalene had already pounced, pushing the whippet onto the ground. 'You? You're looking for the missing? For... for Bob?!'

Count Chocula pushed himself back against a tree, the foliage on his body now strewn across the sand. 'Who is this crazy bitch?'

'My Bob,' said Bwalene, her eyes now red and glinting. 'If you're telling the truth, if you're looking for the missing dogs... take me with you.'

Count Chocula stared at the other dogs, pleading silently as if one of them could stop the wild-eyed Boston. 'You want to come with me?'

Bwalene shook her head. 'No. I *am* coming with you.'

The whippet gazed at the sand. 'Oh. I suppose you are.'

As Bwalene turned and sauntered down to the shore - her shoulders and neck low to the ground - the pug and French bulldog approached Count Chocula.

'She'sth not bad, you know,' said Chompy Chew, nudging the whippet with his spherical head as a gesture of peace. 'It'sth justht that her sthpecial one wasth taken by the gang you're looking for.'

Alfonz nodded. 'Ever since then she's not been the same Bwalene we know and love.' He looked at the whippet sullenly. 'Just a miserable bitch.'

Bwalene's newfound hope was diminishing rapidly as they traversed the undergrowth. She realised the whippet called Count Chocula was – as the islanders called such dogs – a shobstacle. A shit obstacle. Had she stooped so low in her grief to believe such an outlandish tale? A secret mission bestowed upon him by the Council of Greyhounds…

The sky was fading, from amethyst violet to the indigo of a lagoon. Soon there would be no light to guide them.

'I don't believe you,' she said, stopping behind the others.

Chompy Chew was busily snapping mosquitoes out of the air; he stopped, his tongue protruding from one corner of his mouth.

'You come charging out the woods, as clandestine as a flatulent elephant seal, spouting nonsense about a secret mission.' Bwalene could feel a lump in her throat. 'If this is some sort of *weird* game, and believe me, my friends and I find you weird indeed' - the pug and Frenchie found something of great interest on the forest floor -'then tell me now, or so God help me I will do something I'll regret.'

The whippet's mouth hung open. 'Weird?'

Bwalene sighed. 'Alfonz, Chompy, I'm sorry I brought you along. Leave this phoney – he can live out his bizarre fantasies. At least you won't hurt anyone on your own.'

The whippet closed its proboscis. 'I am on a mission,' he said. 'Good day.'

And with that, he turned and left, tripping on a root as he went.

'You did the right thing,' said Alfonz. 'We're here for you. Me and Chompy. We're always here for you, Bwalene.'

She smiled: it took effort, but it was sincere. 'Thank you.'

Chompy Chew looked upward through the gaps in the trees. 'Sthky's getting dark,' he said. 'What sthay we camp down for the night? I could get sthome forethst fruitsth and roathst them on a fire?'

Worry had rendered such concepts as eating irrelevant. Bwalene realised just how hungry she was: her appetite was voracious. The thought of a roast mango set stomach juices in motion, like distant thunder. 'Yes, please. I'm hungrier than I thought.'

Chompy Chew's face brightened. 'Right you are, sthee you in a sthecond.'

Bwalene turned to Alfonz. 'We don't need an incompetent whippet to guide us. We can look for Bob ourselves.' Her stomach rumbled. 'Tomorrow.'

The pug nodded. 'I'll get some firewood.'

Alfonz was skilled in bush-craft; he'd only set fire to himself once, which was a record for the vicinity.

The three companions sat in front of the flames, their shadows casting long, black trails behind them. The forest was alive with the sound of squealing, coughing, hooting, and the occasional fart, the latter of which would silence its occupants, save for the odd chuckle.

'My great, great grandfather found a skeleton in these woods once,' said Alfonz, licking mango juice from his tiny snout. 'It wasn't a dog's. It was wearing clothes; hanging from a branch.'

Bwalene's thoughts drifted away from the conversation. A pang of guilt crawled from the pit of her stomach. She felt she'd been too harsh on Count Chocula. After all, he seemed too stupid to be capable of lying. But then again, Bwalene didn't know what to think anymore. Or who to trust, for that matter.

'I sent him away,' she said, interrupting a debate about where the phalanges resided. 'I've been selfish.'

Chompy Chew leaned towards her, speaking gently. 'Pardon me, Bwalene, but he wasth on his own before he found usth. Besthides, he wasth obviousthly lying.'

'A liar?'

The dogs looked at one another.

'Was that you?' They spoke in unison.

'The Council's finest operative is not a liar.'

They turned round, all of a sudden too aware of the darkness and its encompassing sounds… a frog farted in the distance, but no one laughed.

A large deerhound appeared from the shadows. It was a mangy looking thing - one eye was milky and dead. It grinned: in the darkness it resembled a wolf.

'You're not a liar are you, Count Chocula?' The deerhound peered over his shoulder.

There was a muffled protest; Alfonz, with his keen eyes, thought he could see a shape between the trees.

'Who are you?' said Bwalene. Adrenaline was coursing through her muscles.

'Riptide. Your friend told me a lot about you, before I gagged him and tied him up.' Alfonz flinched as Riptide bared long, curved canines. 'You're looking for… what's the whelp's name now? Bob. It's Bob, isn't it?'

Bwalene's heart sank.

'Do-gooder, as I recall. We've got him back at the camp.'

The Boston terrier's ears flattened. 'Please, please tell me he's okay.' Her words faltered. She tried not to appear weak in front of the beast.

The deerhound clicked his teeth together. 'He's alive, if that's what you mean. Can't say for how long.'

Bwalene launched herself and was knocked to one side, the air from her lungs escaping in a yelp. Chompy Chew ran towards him, narrowly avoiding Riptide's snapping jaws as he slid beneath shaggy legs. The deerhound turned round.

'Where are you, you cleft?' He scanned the darkness. 'If you come out, I promise I won't eat you. Not all of you.'

He chuckled. "Come on, little Frenchie, come out, let Riptide-' The deerhound stopped, suddenly, his grey eyes wide and lips a thin, black line.

He turned. Alfonz was standing with a smouldering branch clenched between his jaws. There was a smell of burnt hair. Riptide whimpered - looked behind him - then ran into the forest, trailed by an orange flicker, his tail wagging frantically between the trees.

Alfonz dropped the branch. 'Is everyone all right?' His voice was shaking.

The others approached him.

'I'm okay,' said Bwalene hoarsely. 'Just a bit winded.'

There was a muffled exclamation in the darkness. 'We'd better free him,' she said. 'And apologise, I suppose.'

Another fart punctuated the darkness; it wasn't a frog.

Count Chocula was not a clever dog, but he had ambition, and that (of course) meant absolutely nothing. This was because an ambitious, incompetent spy was still incompetent. If his chosen career path had been that of – say - a politician, he would have fared better.

But Count Chocula was the universe's answer to stumbling into the right place at the right time. History had a lot of people like this, though they were usually the right people at the wrong time, which explained a lot.

The whippet had managed to guide Bwalene and her companions to the far side of the island, completely by accident.

The Boston terrier seemed more like her old self again in the last week or so. Chompy Chew suspected this had something to do with hope, like finding that bone he'd buried by the cliff edge.

The whippet brought them to the top of a hill – it wasn't as high as the cave of the council, nor as rocky, and there was a path leading to its peak.

A building with a corrugated iron roof stood at its centre; a now defunct cable car which had once travelled down to the canopy by means of a cable rusted nearby.

Alfonz stared at the cable, panting in the way only pugs can, with great difficulty. 'If only it still worked,' he said, his little chest rising and falling rapidly.

Bwalene walked over to the pulley, gripped it with her teeth, and yanked. The cable car gave a great, rusty scream and started to move.

'I forgot there was one of those,' said Count Chocula.

Alfonz did his very best not to bite the whippet.

'This is the old station.' The whippet sniffed at the ancient building. 'This is the founding place, where the Mother lived… or so my uncle says.'

The Mother. Yes – not many dogs had seen her; a solitary figure who wandered the island. She had passed away a few weeks ago, rumour had it.

'This is it,' said Count Chocula, sniffing earnestly at a gap in the wall.

He stuck a paw into the gap and pulled, letting out a deep bark of effort; it was a strange noise to hear from such a wiry, nervous-looking dog.

As he pushed the sliding metal door across – with the help of the other dogs – light poured into the ancient building, launching dust motes into the air, swirling in the golden light.

'An old bloodhound told me about this place,' said Count Chocula, staring into the old laboratory. 'He said there was someone here who could give us answers, someone who knows where the missing dogs are.'

Chompy Chew swallowed and licked his nose. 'The Oracle?'

The whippet nodded, sneezing several times as he

stepped into the dust-filled lab.

'So who is this Oracle?' said Alfonz, staring at a peculiar glass apparatus connected to several other peculiar items. It was as alien to the pug as the concept of socks with sandals.

A rustling sound emanated from the corner of the lab. The dogs turned as one, their teeth bared – all except Bwalene – who tottered over to it, fearlessly. Chompy Chew surmised that any clue, even potentially dangerous ones, might lead her closer to Bob.

The rustling sound grew louder and was followed by 'Huh?' and 'What?'

The Boston terrier approached a low shelf covered with wires and coils. It looked like a makeshift nest; something was in there.

To Chompy Chew, the creature in front of him looked like a tiny dog covered in spikes.

'What? Who are you?' the creature exclaimed. It was very old, with a long, white beard cascading down to its belly.

'We're here to ask you about the Lupine Gang,' said Bwalene with cold determination, 'and about the missing dogs on the island.'

'What? Huh?' said the creature. Alfonz - in his mind - had decided to call it the What-hog.

'I don't know anything about missing dogs.' The creature coughed into its tiny paw. 'But the Lupine Gang... Yes, I could tell you about them, if you like. Very sad... very sad indeed.'

The dogs leaned closer, surrounding the small creature. The What-hog coughed vociferously. 'Very well,' it said, looking at Bwalene's expression - a mixture of hope and sadness.

It told them everything.

*

The first experiments had been a failure. That is to say, in the eyes of the United States Army they had cost too much time and money. What good was espionage if your spy could barely go three feet without taking a piss?

But Professor Hugo Franklin was not the type of person to give up so easily. Something fundamental was missing from his experiment. Some kind of connection that the other test subjects didn't share.

'Alice,' he said, smiling beneath baggy eyes. 'Tell me what you did today, with Sniff.'

The little girl grinned at her father, her legs dangling from the edge of the egg-shaped chair. 'We played catch today, and, and Sniff found an ant hill!' Alice giggled, and the wires on her temples began to blink on and off. 'Sniff got ants in his nose and he sneezed. Achoo! Silly old chicken!'

Hugo watched with great curiosity as the wires on his daughter's head - connected to a tube of shimmering liquid - changed colour. Gold and white, white and gold.

'Alice?' Hugo knew this was what he'd been looking for; this was his answer.

'What, daddy?' said the little girl, grinning with that great gap in her teeth.

'Do you love your doggy? Do you love Sniff?'

Alice nodded fervently. Her fine, blonde hair swooshed in front of her face. 'Yes,' she said. 'I love Sniff. I love Sniff more than the world.' She raised her arms, articulating – as much as a six-year-old can – what it would be like to hug the planet Earth.

'Now, Alice,' said Hugo. 'I want you to close your eyes, go on… take a deep breath, that's it.' He scribbled notes as he spoke. 'Breathe in deeply and relax. I want you to think about Sniff. Really think about him. Think about how much you love him.'

As the girl's belly rose and fell like a sleeping robin's, the wires on her head were no longer intermittent, becoming a solid glow of gold light. The shimmering liquid now shared that strange luminescence.

'Good, Alice,' said the professor. 'I think you may have changed the world.'

The dogs stared at the What-hog, trying to make sense of what the little creature had just told them.

'Alice?' said Bwalene incredulously. 'The Mother?'

The What-hog snorted. 'Yes, I suppose that's what the inhabitants of this island called her.'

'The liquid...' said Alfonz, his gaze turning towards a glass tube. Perhaps it had held the same stuff.

'It's a formula,' said the What-hog, stroking his beard with arthritic hands. 'It's what makes you who you are – or at least, your ancestors. The first test subjects.'

The dogs didn't follow; the What-hog tried to explain.

The formula was used to infuse human consciousness – or perhaps a better way of looking at it was, to instil a higher intelligence or awareness into its test subject. The What-hog had been the first 'animal' to be subjected to it. While the effervescent formula Alice's mind had created had worked, it had also made the What-hog age incredibly slowly, and sleep most of its life away.

'Stho we're the way we are because our ancestorsth were given a formula?' said Chompy Chew, his small brain working overtime.

The What-hog raised a finger. 'Only after the professor had found the right mixture. But what happened, as I've said, was very sad.'

Bwalene pushed her cold, wet, rubbery nose up to the What-hog's face. 'Tell us.'

*

15

Hugo was a man of science, but in these times of nuclear bombs and – a short time later, to Hugo's horror, the discovery of camps that performed sadistic human experiments – he was also a human being and a father.

Although he would come to regret what was to follow, he knew the formula wasn't quite right. Love had created a marvellous concoction, but one with too many extraneous compounds. The excess dopamine, serotonin, diethylamide and God knew how many enzymes had turned the laboratory hedgehog into a somniferous, languid creature. The formula needed a balance; it needed the absence of love.

'Don't want! Don't want this, daddy,' said Alice, wailing into her hands. She was sitting in the egg-shaped chair, tubes connected from her temples to the glass of swirling, gleaming liquid.

'Alice, it's very important we finish this.'

His daughter shook her head stubbornly.

'Close your eyes, Alice… go on… that's it. Take a deep breath.' Hugo pretended to inhale a lungful of air. 'Like that… good. Now, Alice, tell me what happened to Sniff.'

Alice was visibly shaking as tears trickled between her fingers. She spoke in a muffled, toneless voice – a stranger's voice.

'He got his foot caught…' The tears carried on seeping between her fingers, fingers which masked a reddened, contorted face. 'Sniff hurt his leg. He fell down… the hill… he didn't wake up.'

Hugo watched the tubes turn an ugly purple.

'Sniff is dead, isn't he?'

Alice shook her head.

'Yes, Alice, he is.' Hugo watched as the glass of liquid turned from the purple of a bruise to that of an enveloping darkness, swallowing the light like a black hole. 'How does that make you feel, Alice? How does death make you feel?'

The dogs frowned, listening with shock and indignation.

'It wasn't his finest moment,' said the What-hog. 'In fact, shortly after that, he gave up on the experiments entirely.'

Bwalene couldn't shake the image of the crying girl, and the black, abominable liquid. 'Is that who we are?' She was staring at an ancient, dusty glass cylinder. 'Is that what we're made of – the fears of an innocent child?'

The What-hog sighed, his tiny breath blowing the hairs of his beard, like grass beneath a silver moon. 'Yes. And no. The professor mixed the first formula – the golden substance that made me – with the black liquid. The first reactant wasn't right... it was too dark. It was...'

It was all the sadness and grief, all the fear and anxiety and mental anguish the poor girl had suffered. The words didn't need to be said.

'The professor gave that formula to his favourite pet,' said the What-hog.

The laboratory was silent. All eyes were on the small creature.

'Lupine – a husky. Her eyes were beautiful, I'll always remember that: bright blue, like the planet Neptune, as Professor Hugo was wont to say.' The dogs thought they could see a tear – a tiny, sparkling jewel - fall from the corner of the What-hog's eye. 'When the professor administered the formula – not gold, but a dirty, washed out grey, Lupine's eyes changed... it wasn't the colour, it was something in them. As if part of her died.'

The What-hog pointed to the glass tube. 'There were a few dogs, after Lupine. I remember the day she escaped, freeing them from their cages. They are the ancestors of the ones you're looking for, the Lupine Gang.' The What-hog yawned. 'You'll find them north-west of here, in a field of bamboo, by the edge of the cliffs.'

The dogs nodded their thanks and turned to go, but not before the somnolent hedgehog spoke once more. 'There is one other thing…'

'I dreamt of molecules, floating in space. Everything was black, everything was… too big. I woke up feeling suffocated.'

The brown and white spaniel stared at the Boston terrier through bars of bamboo.

'Do you have nightmares?' said the spaniel, looking at the prisoner, with blue and piercing eyes. 'Why do puppies always mewl and cry their hearts out? Hmm? From the very moment we're born into this fragile existence, we are afraid.'

The Boston terrier glanced at the empty bowl by its feet. 'Please… I'm so hungry. It's been days.'

The spaniel smiled - a wooden expression that would have looked more at home on a mannequin. 'And look at you, Bob. Your fear melts away, when the only thing you can think about is food… Survival. Chasing a bitch on heat or gnawing on a thigh bone – these are the things that distract you from your reality. The realisation that we are molecules floating in the vast emptiness, kept together by gravity.'

Bob was beyond 'hangry', he was now bitterly sad and hungry. He was 'had.' 'Go and wax lyrical somewhere else,' he said, his black brow furrowed. 'If you don't have food, I don't care what you have to say.'

The spaniel looked bemused. 'You want me gone? I could go, but it doesn't matter. You will always remember your time here, locked in this cage. That will always be part of your existence, as long as you breathe air and pump blood through your heart. You'll always remember your separation from… what was her name?' The spaniel cocked his head to one side. 'The one you call out to in your sleep… Bwalene?'

Bob snarled, gnashing at the bamboo bars. The spaniel stepped back, his smile never faltering. 'Such a primeval display. So much… energy – but futile, nonetheless. Everything you feel for this Bwalene, it's insignificant.'

Bob licked away blood from his lips; he'd cut his tongue on the bars.

'You will succumb to our ways,' said the spaniel. 'I am doing you a favour, you realise that, don't you?'

The Boston fell back onto his straw bedding.

'We used to transmute dogs without… indoctrination, as you call it,' said the spaniel. 'But grey fusion is temperamental at best. It drives some insane, and - if you're unlucky – it will kill you.'

Bob knew about the grey fusion; he'd been captive for a month now, he'd seen dogs being marched away – returning with a glazed look in their eyes, or not returning at all. If they couldn't break his psyche, they would surely poison him.

'I feel very sorry for you,' he said. 'A life without love is a life not worth living.'

The spaniel stared at the Boston for a long time. His voice was low and full of malice. 'When you lose your mind, when you beg for mercy to have me rip out your throat… I look forward to watching you suffer.'

There was nothing extraordinary about the symbol on the plane. The dogs had no context surrounding the Great War, other than contributing - in some way - to their current awareness. And death, of course. Wherever there was war, death was sure to follow. Far from any conflict, remnants of the war were scattered all over the island.

'Your great, great grandfather wasth right,' said Chompy Chew, looking up at the rusted fuselage.

A skeleton in tattered rags was tangled in the trees by the plane. Its eternal grin was unsettling Alfonz; as if it were reading his mind, laughing at some terrible secret only the pug knew.

'The Council denounced homo sapiens as the dominant race,' said Count Chocula, as if reciting a well versed passage. 'They were the species chosen by evolution. They were tree dwellers, ape-like only a million years ago. For all their enlightenment, my uncle says they still envelop themselves with violence, fear, hatred... greed...'

The whippet drifted off, staring up at the dead Nazi caught in his parachute line.

'Uncle says the slender loris should have been the dominant species.' The whippet's brow creased. 'Something to do with mushrooms... it woke the apes up...' He trailed off again.

'How many daysth journey do you think we have?' said Chompy Chew, swiftly moving on from the whippet's bizarre rantings.

'The What-hog said five days,' said Alfonz looking past the corpse, towards the sun through silhouetted branches. 'It's been... three days, I think.'

The What-hog's revelation had left them with differing emotions. Alfonz had been anxious for the past few days, as if he wasn't really there. He couldn't stop thinking about his own self-awareness; if he thought too hard, he broke into a panic.

Chompy Chew grieved for the girl, Alison. How her father could do a thing like that in the name of science… it made the muscles on his bulbous head flex and tighten.

Bwalene wasn't sure how to feel. The very group she loathed – the Lupine Gang – were victims as well. Nothing was black and white anymore. Well, except for Bwalene of course.

'This... *thing...* is chafing me,' said Count Chocula, adjusting the canvas pack strapped to his back.

Bwalene glared at him. Though she had grown tolerant of the whippet, she still couldn't understand why the Council had picked him. Nepotism seemed to be the only logical answer.

'Let it chafe,' she said. 'You're here to do a job. *Hero.*' Her words were facetious - frustration born of worry. The closer they got to Bob, the greater her trepidation.

The others said nothing. They knew they were close. Count Chocula knew this too; he didn't care about the chafing (not really, anyway) - it was just something to take his mind away from the inevitable.

And if their plan didn't work...

He shook his head, taking one last glimpse at the corpse. The Council had a lot to say about the world beyond the ocean; Count Chocula refused to believe any of it was true.

They moved on. The corpse swayed among the boughs. Even as dusk descended, the creaking of the parachute went long into the night.

The elder greyhound's eyes refracted the firelight, yet even in its orange glow they were cold.

'They're close. Do you feel it?'

Yes. The other members of the Council concurred; it was akin to an imminent storm - a sudden drop in pressure, like something *big* was about to happen.

'Everything is in alignment,' said the sandy-haired greyhound. Her eyes met the elder's – they too were cold.

No one spoke. They didn't need to; they understood. It was incommunicable. They were, after all, ancestors of the enlightened ones: the lucky brothers and sisters of the failed experiments, the Lupine Gang.

After a time, the greyhound with the shining, brown coat looked at his brethren. 'We can see into the fire. We can see the very elements – the fabric of consciousness and all things that transcend this density...' His eyes were not cold, they were infinitely bemused. 'But I still don't understand... Why Count Chocula?'

The sunset was beautiful; Bwalene always remembered that. They'd crested an incline, gazing at the bamboo forest below. And the sunset was beautiful.

The dogs at the bottom of the hill, the dogs barking at the caged prisoners and indoctrinating them with their nihilism – they saw the sunset every day no doubt, but they would never feel the beauty that coursed through Bwalene's body.

We were an experiment, she thought, as her companions - the pug and French bulldog – padded along beside her. Chemicals in a tube.

On the day Bwalene was on the beach, unable to feel the sun on her skin, or the sand between her paws... that was how it felt, to be one of the Lupine Gang.

It was clear to the Boston terrier why they had taken the other dogs; why they had taken Bob. They wanted them to understand what it was like - to feel fear, sadness, emptiness... nothingness. Somehow the Mother (once a little girl named Alice) had kept them at bay. Had kept peace.

Maybe it was because she understood. Maybe it was because it was her pain they were sharing.

Bwalene could see some of the dogs concentrated around a pool of water. That was good. She hoped the whippet had been successful; it was such an outlandish plan, but what other choice did they have?

The Boston terrier waited for a long time, making sure the dogs that weren't in cages had - at one point or another that evening - gone to the watering hole. It was almost dark when Bwalene called out.

'LISTEN, AND LISTEN WELL! THIS STOPS NOW!'

Eyes looked up, followed by an assortment of teeth.

'I'm sorry for the way you feel,' she called, as a Doberman came marching towards her. 'I'm sorry the Mother has lost her influence on you.'

The Lupine Gang's ears seemed to prick, each and every one of them.

'You are all victims,' she said, 'because of the mistakes of others.' She could see Count Chocula creeping up the incline, partly obscured by the bamboo, a glass vial in his mouth. She smiled. 'But you no longer have to live like this.'

Count Chocula reached the summit, dropping the vial on the ground. He'd done it! The clumsy, stupid, wonderful whippet had actually done it!

'He kept the formula,' the What-hog had said, pointing to a large, silver fridge.

It had been a parting gift, Bwalene realised - the formula. The one Alice had created as she thought about her dog, Sniff, of the profound connection they'd shared. An ineffable love.

And there was the answer. It opened like a lotus in Bwalene's mind.

There were chemicals in the mind, yes – there was a science to it, but there was something else in her awareness, the awareness all the dogs on the island experienced. It was something the professor had used (a key) to unlock his life's work. It was the indescribable feeling of love – a force that smashed atoms and created worlds, which allowed consciousness to experience itself in all its awe.

And then... the formula Count Chocula had poured into the watering hole was taking its effect. The Lupine Gang opened their eyes for the first time, and they were no longer afraid.

The What-hog woke from one of its many slumbers, returning to the waking world from a dream that was... more a memory. One that was not his own.

'Alice?' he called, and then realised where he was. He fell back to sleep, into the memory of that other.

The old woman coughed as she knelt amongst the bamboo by the watering hole.

'My time is almost up,' she said, smiling faintly.

The dogs behind her who, by their very nature, were melancholic, seemed gloomier as they watched the Mother. She was dying; they felt it.

'I forgive you dad,' said Alice, removing a silver chain from her neck. 'But you know that already, don't you?'

A tear fell. She placed the necklace on Hugo Franklin's grave.

'You gave this to me.'

The necklace had a pendant of a small dog, silver inlaid with sapphire.

'You made this island,' said Alice, wiping away her tear. 'This island of smoothies. And I wouldn't take back a moment of it. They are my family.' She closed her eyes. 'So this is my gift to you, dad. I forgive you; I love you and I always have and always will. Because that's all that matters to me. That and the smoothies.'

She put her hand on the necklace. Behind her, muzzles appeared one by one, and licked her hand.

The What-hog stirred in his sleep, smiling.

*

Alfonz, Chompy Chew and Count Chocula were running across the sand, doing what dogs do best... living their lives, and occasionally, sniffing one another's bottoms.

The beach was busy today; several other dogs had joined them. They were enjoying the the sun on their backs, the way the sand poured between their paws, and the smell of the jungle - earthy and green, with hints of flatulence.

They no longer had a name for themselves. They just *were*, and more importantly, they were happy. Especially Old Marvin: the bloodhound lay snoring beneath a pine tree, tendrils of tobacco dangling from his nostrils.

Strange noises were emanating from a side room in the laboratory: sounds of pleasure and exultation. The What-hog was sure he didn't want to know.

Bwalene and Bob were certainly having fun; Bob had found the old professor's stash of chocolate.

The two dogs chomped and chewed, smacking their jowls with sounds of euphoria – the kind only chocolate, and perhaps a few other things, can bring.

Words were meaningless in moments like these. The joy they felt could only be expressed through chomping and chewing. Food - after all - was a dog's best friend.

It was a happy ending. Apart from the chocolate of course. It was going to be a noisy night.

ABOUT THE AUTHOR

Max Sandall received a BA (Hons) in Creative Writing at the University of Gloucestershire in 2009. He contributed to the short story collections, *The Redundancy of Flightless Birds* and *Standing in the Kitchen at Parties* (published by Deserted By Dignity) in 2010 and 2011 respectively. He lives in Gloucestershire, surrounded by smoothies.

4887529GR00021

Made in the USA
Charleston, SC
12 November 2015